Not Your Happy Dance

poems by

Ryan Scariano

Finishing Line Press
Georgetown, Kentucky

Not Your Happy Dance

Copyright © 2021 by Ryan Scariano
ISBN 978-1-64662-436-2 First Edition
All rights reserved under International and Pan-American Copyright Conventions. No part of this book may be reproduced in any manner whatsoever without written permission from the publisher, except in the case of brief quotations embodied in critical articles and reviews.

ACKNOWLEDGMENTS

With much gratitude for the editors of the following journals, anthologies, and websites in which these poems first appeared, many in earlier versions.

Basalt: "Certainly" and "Grace"
Bright Bones: Contemporary Montana Writing: "Bruised Muse" and "My Warmest Coat"
Fault Lines: "Not Your Happy Dance"
Hair of the Dog: An Anthology: "Pawing the Door"
Heart of the Rat: An Anthology: "Rat (Rattus Norvegicus)"
Ink Node: "Pickling Song," "The Worst Winter Since 1989," "Black Friday Night," and "Feeling Deeply"
Oklahoma Review: "Late-Night, 395 South"
Paper Nautilus: "Northern Flicker"
Phantom Drift: "Marmot Road"
Rock & Sling: "Dear Jonah"
The American Journal of Poetry: "The Dragon in the Room"
Thunder Sandwich: "Every Time You Leave"
Verde Que Te Quiero Verde: Poems after Federico Garcia Lorca: "The Old Country"
Verde Que Te Quiero Verde: Poems after Federico Garcia Lorca, 2nd Edition: "What You Mean is the Ritual"
We All Lived Here (The MFA at EWU's Alumni Publishing Project): "Mohamed Upstairs"

Additionally, "Black Friday Night" also appeared in *Railtown Almanac: A Spokane Poetry Anthology* and at RadicalDivorce.com.

And finally, "Not Your Happy Dance" and "Every Time You Leave" also appeared in the chapbook, *Smithereens*, published by Imperfect Press.

Publisher: Leah Maines
Editor: Christen Kincaid
Front Cover Art: FreeVintageArt.com
Back Cover Art: "Phantoms foot it to the Death-watch drum." From *Episodes of Insect Life* by Acheta Domestica (a.k.a. L. M. Budgen), 1851.
Cover Design: Elizabeth Maines McCleavy
Author Photo: Beth C. Ford

Order online: www.finishinglinepress.com
also available on amazon.com

Author inquiries and mail orders:
Finishing Line Press
P. O. Box 1626
Georgetown, Kentucky 40324
U. S. A.

Table of Contents

Hum

A Messy Picnic 1
Letting the Evening Come.. 2
Late-Night, 395 South 3
Pickling Song 4
Not Your Happy Dance.. 5
Marmot Road 6
Certainly.. 7
Bruised Muse 8
With the Insects... 9
What You Mean is the Ritual 10
The Old Country 11
My Warmest Coat.. 12
Dear Jonah... 13
Prayer for the Commencement of… 14
The Lilac.. 15

Black

The Dragon in the Room.. 19
Northern Flicker.. 20
Brown... 21
Every Time You Leave... 22
Pawing the Door.. 23
The Worst Winter Since 1989 24
Rat (Rattus Norvegicus) 25
Black Friday Night... 26
Mohamed Upstairs.. 27
Vernal... 28
The First Warm Day Since She Left............................... 29
Grace 30
To Vinegar at Summer's End.. 31
Feeling Deeply... 32
Still the Wave... 33

Hum

A Messy Picnic

I spread out a messy picnic to see yellowjackets dance with the sticky tub of precut pineapple, to see little ants flirt with the chips, to see a big ant fall into my beer, to see gnats wasted on my wine. The hum and buzz of this chemical language makes me wonder: what kind of insect am I? —drunk on sharing when everyone has left the park. Now I find *here* and *there* and *crumb* and *moonlight* and *damp*.

Letting the Evening Come

Like dad out of work. Like the backyard.
Like the old German lady who lived in the bramble.
Like an opossum or a stray. Like spare change.
Like a paper route. Like high school. Like a car
and a party. Like a reliable connection.
Like the smoky windows and creamy leather interior
of a Cadillac. Like a dark road. Like losing
the bullet. Like beating a rap. Like winning a bet.
Like filet and lobster tail. Like taking
French leave French wine French kiss.
Like a renaissance. Like you always knew the way
home. Like the belly of a beautiful woman. Like a cat.
Like bone china. Like a cup of tea. Like walking along
the sound. Like sea glass and tumbled stones.
Like returning to the hummingbird and a wet garden.
Like clover. Like a pear tree. Like a blanket and a rainbow.
Like letting the evening come. Like the moment
and its spell of stillness under which we fall.

Late-Night, 395 South

Like never before
and never again
Muse Road snuck up
out of the fog
and kissed me.

Pickling Song

She's washing Mason jars, cutting dill,
scrubbing cucumbers, bringing the brine
to a boil. It's a process. A short season's
worth of salt. A sea of apple cider vinegar.
She's hearing the song. I peel the garlic
from her mother's garden. Fat, earth
encrusted bulbs cling to thick fibrous necks.
The largest cloves slip from their papery skins
polished white jade wet with green light.
She's puzzled the cucumbers into their shells,
and now, in flows her brine. I twist on the lids,
flip the jars and line them up along the edge
of the great countertop. The hum of an ancient
mantra presses through the half-smile
of her lips. I've almost made out the melody.

Not Your Happy Dance

Do that cute little dance for me—
not your happy dance—the goofy little rumpus
that you bust out on extra-special occasions,
when entirely delighted, when you hum created,
the one you haven't thrown down
for many souls. You know, that secret little bounce
and wiggle, head cocking from side to side,
that perfect shimmy, that sacred hustle,
when you puff your cheeks, roll your eyes and make
those tiny squeaks in the back of your throat.
I know you feel silly when I ask for it,
but now that you've shown me,
there's not a whole lot else I can do.

Marmot Road

Trying to get to Nate's place,
I turned on Marmot Road
when I should've stayed
on Ten Eyck to Bull Run.
I wound through the forest
broken by wet pasture and Holsteins,
past a barn leaning against
a hand-lettered sign for eggs.
Though I knew I was lost, I hummed
along the Devil's Backbone
with the big river on one side
and the little river on the other.
My ears popped. The moss
and lichen flashed like sunshine
in my eyes. Was I driving toward
the original marmot still
dreaming in his burrow
by a secret clear lake?
But there never have been
marmots in these parts.
Night fell and I broke down
by the muddy roadside creek.
Yet, as the moon clouded,
this sad trickle off the mountain
eased through a culvert and pooled
in a brownish-black puddle
amid cedar and hemlock.
My dark earth was ripe with
the fertile scents.
Here the primordial mountain beaver
found me. Unexpectedly,
I prayed to her for ten million years
as she counted her stars
and ate fiddleheads.

Certainly

Something shiny catches my eye
as I cross the street to the car—
a scuffed, little disco ball bead.
I toss it into the ashtray, next to
the tooth-sized piece of quartz,
the starry green shard of sea glass,
the paperclip, and two
new pennies. Certainly
I am becoming a crow.

Bruised Muse

You sing along the rained and rutted
highway heading south. On a hotel bed
in Kennewick, I write you down.
Your eyes hazel out into infinity:
help me craft it. Help me string words
and twine spiral spokes of the galaxy
in your breath. Help me polish these syllables.
Tell me how much it reminds you. Tell me
it makes you think of Hafiz. Unpack your Hafiz.
You are the poem. When I'm with you,
you sing along. I tear off pieces
and carry them away.

With the Insects

The creek laughs
and I drop the book
and the praying
mantis winks
and I raise my hands like
I'm testifying
or under arrest
and I shiver and tingle
and weep and breathe
and the dark behind my eyelids
glitters
and all this
lasts for only
a few moments.

What You Mean is the Ritual

Notice the spider's thread holding
everything in place.
What you mean is the way
skunk and coyote
create the night on your street,
the way crow and squirrel dream
daylight in your yard.
It's the ritual you mean,
that fondness pressing your life
into grassy lawn, touching your death
to each cool stone. What you mean—
we have access without pretense
on the trail, in the creek,
with the earth.
This old new land is personal.

The Old Country

When they trepanned me, I saw blue, green, yellow,
and violet over the gray hill, past the river of history beating
enormous and copper. Folk from the bloody town
fill their pockets with pennies. No one returns.
The old country is where they go, if you believe
the postcards, which say that even though the old country
is bloody just like our town, and the ash of revolution clouds
every fiery sunset, still you can hear a song
in each cold kernel of glass. A bloody song with a bloody chorus.
So why do the townspeople descend into the copper mine?
Why are their postcards so jubilant? I have pennies in a pickle jar.
They belonged to my grandmother. Her thoughts are rusting
through my eyes. The ochre in my lungs, the lacquer
on my bones. The people in my town and those who left
are humming. I taste iron and clay mud. I smell roses
and rotting wood.

My Warmest Coat

She knocked on my door
one winter night
in the middle of last summer,
placed a call, powdered
her button nose,
used my convenience,
and when I left the parlor
to still and quiet the kettle,
she stole my only goat,
led him off at the end
of my favorite rope.
My *favorite* rope.
She eloped into the cold
oak forest and all I could hope
was that she'd also stolen
my warmest coat.

Dear Jonah

It's been eons since we last saw each other.
I hope your weather's fair and that you're coming up
for air every once in a while. I'm well enough, or at least,
I shouldn't complain. Although, beyond your presence,
it seems I'm just going through the motions, feeling perfectly
uninhabited. When I finally realized how much of our whole mess
was my fault, my life became a held breath, ash and hollow prayers.
In retrospect, it's obvious I had no control over my actions.
How little control we ever have over anything! I starve
for the time we shared. I miss the scent of you, the taste.
And I still stand by my claim that God made you
for me. You should be living your life much closer to my heart.
Letting you get away was a blunder of biblical proportions.
I truly hope you're happy. I also hope my dropping this line
into the depths of the past doesn't upset you, but I'm compelled
to make contact, to tell you that you've never left my thoughts.
I wish you the best. I don't know why it's been so hard,
and taken me so long, to say those words. Anyway, please
be careful with yourself, and please let me know
how the big salty blue is treating you. Yours forever.

**Prayer for the Commencement of
Our Annual Journey to Ikea
to Stock Up on Tea Lights**

O great and mighty Tea Light Candle,
may the infinitely soft yet wholly
soul searing light of your flame
be eternally aglow. May the other gods
keep you watchful and steadfast company
as we implore your guidance
in this year's tea light
harvest. Godspeed in our love
and veneration, Godspeed
on our journey.

The Lilac

her loamy eyes welled this scent this sweet chill
a story the bees tell before sunset adrift in the air

toward the trembling diamond spider web and back
this lilac breeze a memory whispered once

by our mother the coffin's promise of a land
where nothing goes to waste this buzz of spring this stumble

the fingers of the lawn reaching past the hawthorn
through the elm's papery fruit the lilac's little trumpets

pouring forth damp light flush with chlorophyll
honeyed and ascending to purple soft as satin trim

Black

The Dragon in the Room

> *I keep looking for dragons in this country, and not finding any.*
> —Ursula K. Le Guin

First, eat the damned elephant taking up too much space. Eat the windows and the walls, the sundry items in the closets and the cupboards. Eat the computers and the phones. Eat the houseplants and the gardens. Eat the chickens. Eat the pets. Eat the hummingbirds and the butterflies. Eat the poor, the cold, the huddled, the hungry. Especially eat the hungry. You're hungry. You're cold and tired. You're huddled all by yourself. Eat the rust on your belly. Eat the mold and grime webbing your claws. Eat the raw data oozing from your pores. Eat the invoices and the taxes. Eat the tithes paid in kind. Eat the churches and the truck stops, the airports and the junkyards. Eat the billboards. Eat the casinos. Eat the prayers and the spells and the songs. Eat the receipts. Let everything else burn.

Northern Flicker

The snow whispers a lesson
in letting go. The leaves
are shouting
from brown and gold
to green and greener. They fall
clear up into the sky. The flicker
flares so brightly I can hear
in my dark the flame he carries
underwing, diving from pine
to ash. I drink myself dumb
on the back porch, wait all
evening for the spark to leap
from that damned flicker.
When it does, it lands
in my cocktail, hissing
against the ice just as you call
to say you wish
I had driven over. Temptation
speeds across the state, slams
head-on into my slur.
Now hear me search for and
curse the landmarks in my dark.
Listen to the radio signal
break apart. I'm roaring off
into a midnight blackout.

Brown

All you could possibly have inside of you
is my big yawning black hole and my black eye.
I'm writing this in black ink. Kiss me
with those black eyelashes. Your mascara
runs but can't hide from that black eye
inside. My fingertips turn black, and my outlook
on escaping the gravitational pull of loneliness
bleakly hangs on, and yes, it's also black. So, I sip
from the black cup and swing from the cusp
of a bright black moon. Black caws wheel
with the crows in a black sky. The black smell
of the black tide beckons. Even the air I breathe
blackens as I wait for you to ignite my cell
with your text. I'm nothing if not devoted
to want, to inspiration anywhere other
than you. This poem isn't about you.
But it's still about want. It hardly moves.
Or if it does, it twists around the I. Not your eyes.
I want everything in this black universe
except you and your brown eyes that grow
innocent and light when you bring them close.

Every Time You Leave

It's not that I'm squalid alone, but rather
that soon after every time you leave,
those tiny black sugar ants emerge
from the gaps and cracks, from inside the walls
and from under the house, to mock you.
Little seasonal keystrokes, they strike across
the countertop a jumbled diatribe,
a continuous scurried rail against our order,
never suspecting your blazing return,
never tiring of the lineup for your sweet
sticky poison and your bleach-soaked rag.

Pawing the Door

She turned on the light in her heart, then sent me back
into the dark. I drove in circles, corkscrewing into winter.
There are as many animals here as in the dreams of a child.
Barn owl, coyote, mule deer, mouse, raccoon,
cold cat under the porch, they see one another in this
moonless night, moving through the trees and around the edges
of the yard. Yet, up the icy steps I scramble and hope.
Her heart glows, and I find a place once again with my brother
the dog. Ours is to bark and yowl, paw the door, knowing
there is warmth within.

The Worst Winter Since 1989

For the past three days,
white wind and heavy drifts
have closed the road.
Besieged by ten below,
but there's enough to eat
and the power has held.
Then a strange miracle rises
from beneath this rented house,
from beneath winter—
the green sound of tree frogs.
I work into the night
deciphering the offer—
an invitation for escape
down to their abode,
to clamber amid the rotting
foundation, to sit
in their muddy rooms,
anoint myself
at their mystical font,
take communion
of spider beetle moth,
to be for a moment
born again.

Rat (Rattus Norvegicus)

On his coat of arms the wormy apple
and barn cat. His robes of night so royal
the purple's black. Herald of science,
prophet of medicine, in the corner of my eye
he sees his reflection. At arm's length
he's kept me his cousin.

My cousin always building his nest
within the pink sound of my voice.
My heavy sleep a crumb-like gift,
a winter dream in the pantry,
the only song I have for sharing
this warmth in the walls.

Black Friday Night

My jade plant start loves the logic
of streetlamps. She wants to prosper,
to grow under the moonlight.
She wants to shine off the gleam
in the snow. She feels what I feel
burning in the soft electric glow
from the Christmas lights
across the road. She wants to bloom.
For her, during even the darkest
hours, I will leave up the blinds.
She wants to sing her delicate white
stars through my steamy window
and out into the midnights of
a new year.

Mohamed Upstairs

The upstairs neighbor,
Mohamed, welcomed me
when I moved into the building.
Maqluba, kabsa, kanafeh.
Mohamed upstairs
in that little apartment
with his pregnant wife
and three young daughters.
Mohamed in the laundry room.
Mohamed fetching his children
home from school.
Mohamed working
the graveyard shift.
Maqluba, kabsa, kanafeh.
Mohamed smoking on the stoop.
Mohamed waiting for spring.
Maqluba, kabsa, kanafeh.
Mohamed upstairs cooking,
and I'll make a gift
for his new son, a suncatcher
shining with bits of glass,
green, brown, and blue.
Maqluba, kabsa, kanafeh.
My friend, Mohamed,
knocking at the door with food,
teaching me the names of his dishes.

Vernal

If I don't tell her
She's not a cherry blossom,
That early morning moth
Fluttering in the small white breeze
Might get the wrong idea
And become a tree.

The First Warm Day Since She Left

This morning I see in wavering degrees
the green, yellow, and brown that stitches
the breeze to hay field. I see rush grass
married to wire fence's drunken lean,
and the wounded heart on blackbird's
sleeve. I see scarecrow proposing
to farmhouse, and tractor pining
for dinosaur. I see the tumbleweed beards
of the oncoming men in their trucks.
I see the mountains behind the mountains.

Grace

Heavenly father and mother, sister and brother,
O great and wise aunt and laughing uncle,
thank you for bringing us to your table.
Please watch over us from this moment
forward. Guide us and our many long-lost
cousins through day and night. Allow us
to hear the song and smell the stove. Nourish
our desire to share. Help us in our gratitude
for the things we hold. Help us in our gratitude
for the thing belonging to all. Witness
our awe at being and having been. We implore you.
Grant us a sip from the cup of your grace.
Also, in your absolute wisdom,
we beseech your mercy on behalf
of the lion that would eat us for his dinner;
for we know his hunger is our own. Together
at your table we give thanks for this
divine hello and goodbye. Amen.

To Vinegar at Summer's End

With your pale light, you shroud
the dying world, remember us
in our prime. And I
who must continually obsess
over the zeros, owe to you
the rarest number. I imagine
a million years ago,
one of the drunken mothers figured
you had taken the wine and turned
against her. But then her bones told her,
your sour disposition—
accepting a yellowed memory
in place of green life—
was the only way
to obscure black time.
O Vinegar, I finally appreciate
how you inhale summer's glow
and exhale that long amber breath.

Feeling Deeply

If only you could choose
to feel deeply. Since you cannot,
I will feel deeply for us both.
I will bury our hundred summers
in a hole far away.
Like ten thousand miles.
Like I thought I knew
the way home. Like Bull thistle
Russian thistle blood thistle ghost thistle.
Like puncture vine and yellow star.
Like the wishes and curses
I keep in a tiny jar inside
the jar where you keep me. Like my echoing
pleas for mercy and comprehension.
Like the absence of your feeling
pulling me. Like a limping
waltz. Like a rainy man
forced off a homeless corner.
Like Irish whiskey and Xanax bars,
and tar heroin smoked on tin foil.
Like the foggy hawk wrecked
in the gravelly shoulder and then
the dead doe in the curve and the fawn
dead on the next curve. Like the wrens
that made their nest
in the battery compartment
of the weed whacker
and the mother's quiet black eyes
when we discovered her.
Like she pleaded for our mercy
and comprehension.
I will not wake from this grief,
except with words
pushing through the soil
into the light
of my bluest room.

Still the Wave

There's still a wave
from the old men
in their new trucks,
still the eyelevel
fencepost hawks,
still the lonely elk,
still the field
where I always hear
but never see
the meadowlark,
still my passing by
the creosote-colored mare
on the sunny side
of the barn.
From the look in her eye,
I think she knows
she grazes on
my miles.
When she nuzzles
my thoughts,
rain and earth mix
into muddy milk.
I drink it in
and drive farther
down the road.

Ryan Scariano is the author of *Smithereens*, published by Imperfect Press. His poetry has appeared in *The American Journal of Poetry, Rock & Sling, Phantom Drift, basalt, the Oregonian, Criminal Class Review, J Journal: New Writing on Justice, Paper Nautilus, Thunder Sandwich* and other places. He's been anthologized in *Bright Bones: Contemporary Montana Writing; Verde Que Te Quiero Verde: Poems after Federico Garcia Lorca; Railtown Almanac: A Spokane Poetry Anthology;* the Willow Springs Books anthologies, *Hair of the Dog* and *Heart of the Rat*; and elsewhere.

He lives in La Grande, Oregon. Find him online at *ryanscariano.com*.

www.ingramcontent.com/pod-product-compliance
Lightning Source LLC
LaVergne TN
LVHW041556070426
835507LV00011B/1116